Do You Know?

HOW ANIMALS LIVE

By
Philip Steele
Illustrated by
Bob Bampton

A Piccolo
Piper Book

Contents

In this book you can find out about thirteen different animals and how they live. You can discover how a crocodile hides her eggs and how a hermit crab finds a home.

It is very important that we should find out how creatures live from day to day. Animals are not oddities from zoos and circuses. They are our relatives. We must share this planet with them.

Although we are the most intelligent beings on Earth, we do not treat our fellow creatures very well. We hunt whales and elephants, for example, just because of our greed for money.

Every year more and more people are born into the world. They need to be fed, and so wild country is being turned into farmland. They need to have houses, so our cities spread into the countryside. They need to work, so factory waste poisons the land.

Many animals find it hard to survive in our world. We must learn to help them – or we may lose our best friends.

1 All Kinds Of Animals

Did you know that there are over a million different kinds of animals in the world? There are tiny beetles only a ¼ of a millimetre long, and there are giants such as the blue whale, which can be as long as 34 metres.

Over the ages our planet has gone through many changes. Animals have had to change too in order to survive. If they cannot find food or if the climate

The horse in this picture is a *mammal*, like us. Its body produces heat to stay warm, and it feeds its young on its own milk. The flycatchers below are *birds.* They are covered in feathers and lay eggs. The *insects* on the leaves also lay eggs, and they change their shape as they grow. There are more insects in the world than all the other animals put together.

suddenly changes, they die out altogether. The giraffe has survived by growing a long neck, so that it can eat leaves from the tree-tops. The tiger has survived by growing sharp teeth to kill its prey.

Over the years scientists have divided all the different animals into groups of creatures that have developed in similar ways. This helps us to tell one animal from another.

Snakes belong to a group known as *reptiles.* Reptiles are egg-laying creatures, covered in tough pieces of skin called scales. This carpet python is protecting its eggs.

Newts are *amphibians.* They can live on land and in the water. The stickleback below it lives only in water. It is a *fish.* Fish breathe under water through flaps in their sides, called gills.

There are also all kinds of small creatures which belong to different groups. The snail, for example, is a *mollusc.* The earthworm is an *annelid.* Both of these are boneless creatures.

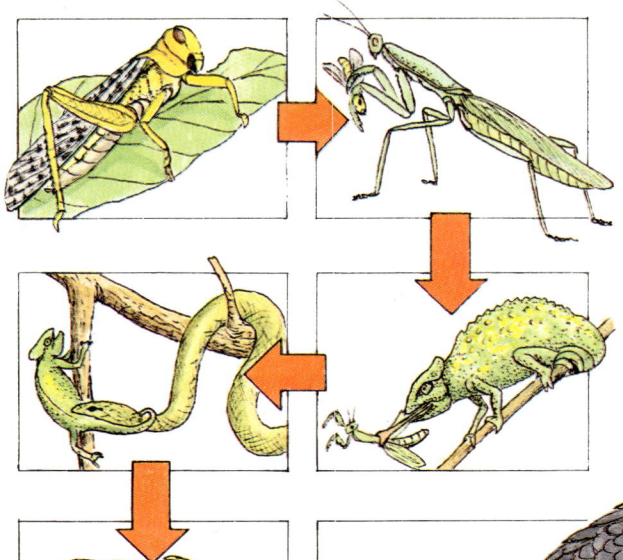

All living things, whatever group they belong to, depend for their survival on the Sun. The Sun makes plants grow, and animals eat the plants. The plant-eating animals are then eaten by other animals. For example, a leaf-eating locust is eaten by a mantis. The mantis is caught by a chameleon, which is in turn eaten by a snake. The snake is attacked by a mongoose, which is killed by an eagle. Finally, the remains of dead animals enrich the soil and so help new plants to grow.

2 The Hermit Crab

In a rockpool you will find many different kinds of animals living closely together within a small area. You might find starfish (1), water insects, small fish, barnacles (2) and shrimps.

You are sure to find some shellfish. These belong to the group of animals known as molluscs. Some molluscs, like the limpet (3), surround their bodies with a single shell. Others, like the mussel (4), have a shell made of two sections.

Crabs belong to the group of creatures we call *crustaceans.* Instead of having their skeletons inside their bodies they wear them outside, like armour-plating. But there is a kind of crab that no longer has armour on its back at all. Only its legs and the front part of its body are protected. This crab is called the hermit crab (5).

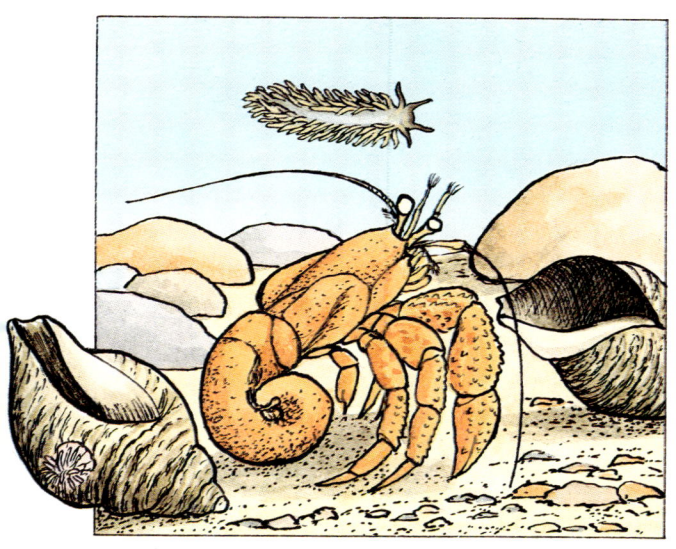

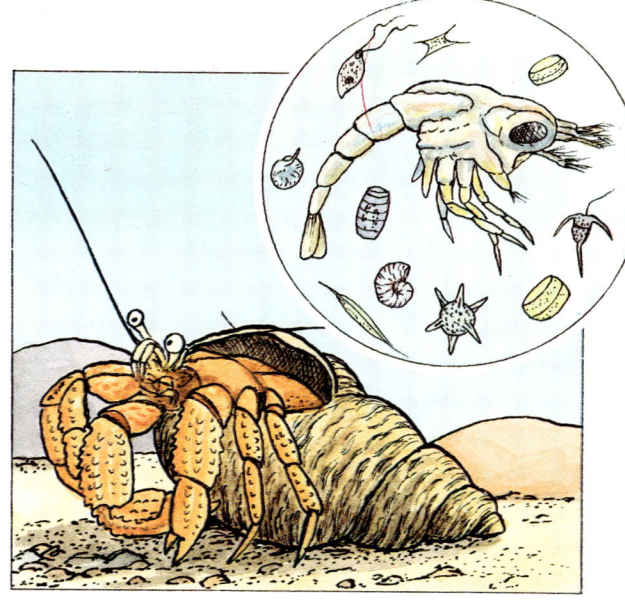

Most crabs live safely inside their armour. But hermit crabs have to protect the soft part of their bodies in a different way. They do this by squeezing into the shell of a dead mollusc such as a whelk. As hermit crabs grow bigger, they have to crawl out of the first shell and find a larger one. This is a dangerous time for the unprotected crab.

A female hermit crab will lay thousands of eggs, which she carries in her shell until they hatch into larvae. These tiny transparent creatures float about in the water with other microscopic plants and animals. When it is big enough, the young crab sinks to the ground to find itself a shell to live in.

A hermit crab often shares its home with other sea creatures. Barnacles and plant-like animals called sea anemones will cling to the outside of the shell. In return for this hospitality, the anemone's stinging tentacles help to protect the crab from its enemies. Bristleworms may even live in the shell. As the crab feeds, all these 'lodgers' are able to pick up scraps of food too.

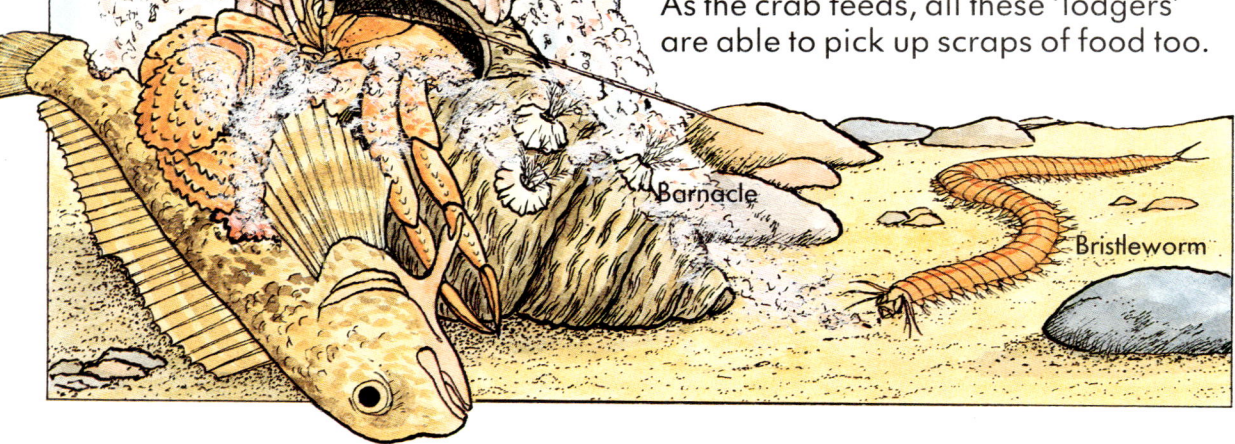

Sea anemone

Barnacle

Bristleworm

3 The Common Frog

Frogs and toads belong to the group of animals we call amphibians. The common frog is typical of its kind. It is a small, smooth, damp-skinned creature that eats slugs, snails and worms. And the long sticky tongue which shoots out of its wide mouth is ideal for catching insects.

The common frog mates in the spring. The female lays thousands of tiny eggs in ponds and ditches. The eggs are covered in jelly. They swell up in the water and soon rise to the surface, where they stick together in clusters known as frogspawn. Before the spawn turns into adult frogs it goes through several changes.

The eggs turn into tadpoles. At first a tadpole is all head and tail. It looks rather like a small dark fish. Like a fish, the tadpole breathes through gills. These take oxygen out of the water. But much of the frogspawn and many of the tadpoles are eaten by water birds and other pond creatures before they have the chance to grow into frogs.

At the age of five weeks the tadpole starts growing back legs. Inside its body lungs are forming, and before long it can breathe in air from the surface. At ten weeks the front legs grow and the tail starts to disappear. The tadpole is turning into a frog.

When it is three months old, the baby frog is able to leave the pond. It takes in oxygen through its lungs and through its skin. The young frogs make an attractive meal for many other creatures. They need their long back legs to leap away.

There are about 1800 different kinds of frogs and toads in the world. Some live in marshes and others in trees. Some protect themselves by changing colour. One South American frog makes a deadly poison which the Choco Indians put on their arrows.

Toads are first cousins to the frogs. You can tell the difference by the toad's rougher, drier skin. The common toad, like many frogs, sleeps through the winter. During the mating season, the male croaks, puffing up its throat. The female lays eggs in long chains.

The Atlantic Salmon

In August or September you might see a beautiful silver fish as it leaps up a waterfall or a river weir. The Atlantic salmon is battling its way upstream. It is going back to the place where it was born.

Most fish live either in rivers and lakes or in the sea. The salmon can do both. It starts life in fresh water, but later it swims out to sea, travelling thousands of kilometres.

The life story of the Atlantic salmon begins in the rivers of western Europe and northeastern America. The female digs out a nest, called a redd, in the gravel of the river bed. Here she lays her eggs, which are fertilized by the male.

The eggs hatch out into baby fish called alevins. They are less than 1½ centimetres long. They are still attached to the yolk sac of the egg, and this gives them food. For six weeks or so the alevins hide in the pebbles on the river bed.

At 2½ centimetres long the baby salmon are known as fry. They swim about freely, eating tiny water creatures. As they grow bigger they turn into parr. Black spots appear on their sides.

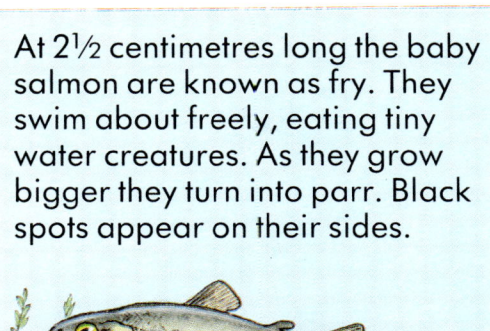

By their second year the young fish are about 15 centimetres long. Sooner or later their scales turn silver. These smolt swim to the river mouth and then out into the Atlantic Ocean.

At sea, the salmon feed on small fish and crustaceans. They soon grow and after three years they can be over a metre long.

Some salmon stay in saltwater for only a year. Others stay for up to four years. Then they go back to their home river. Without stopping to feed, they race upstream to breed. Most salmon then die, but a few live to make the journey a second time.

Today, the salmon are disappearing. We block salmon rivers with dams and poison the water with waste. Salmon are popular as food, too, and we catch them in large numbers.

⑤ The Wood Ant

Have you ever seen a mound of pine needles in the woods? They could mark the site of a wood ant's nest. Below the needles lie a maze of tunnels and underground chambers.

The red and black wood ant is typical of the group of animals we call insects. Its body is formed in three parts. First, there is the head, which carries a pair of feelers called antennae. The second part, the middle, is called the thorax and has three pairs of legs attached to it. The rear part of the body is the abdomen.

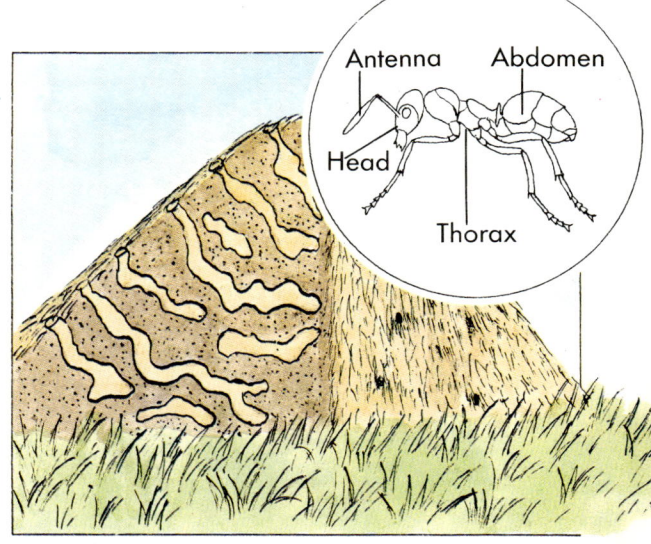

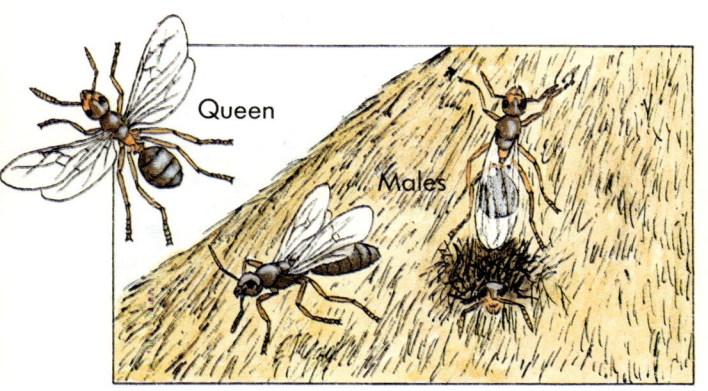

Queen

Males

There are three kinds of wood ant – the queen, the male and the worker. Only the worker has no wings. The queen is chased by the males on a wedding flight. When she lands, she mates with a male, then loses her wings and crawls into an underground chamber. Here she lays her eggs. The males all die after the mating flight.

The eggs are carried off by the worker ants – small females which cannot breed. The eggs hatch as grub-like larvae and are fed by the workers until they turn into adults.

Queens can carry on producing eggs for up to fifteen years without ever leaving the underground chamber again. So one nest may contain as many as 100,000 ants. With so many ants, the nest has to be very well organized. Workers go off to search for food outside the nest. They mark their route with a strong scent so that other ants can follow. Columns of ants stream back and forth.

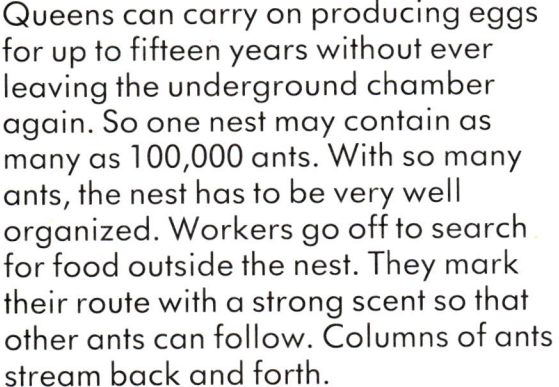

Most ants will eat almost anything. Other insects, scraps of leaves and seeds are all dragged or carried back to the nest as food.

Wood ants are fierce creatures. They will attack animals bigger than themselves and will squirt acid and bite. An ant recognizes others from its own nest by their smell. By touching antennae ants can pass information to each other. Ants are useful insects, as they destroy pests that may otherwise harm the trees. The wood ants' main enemy is the woodpecker.

13

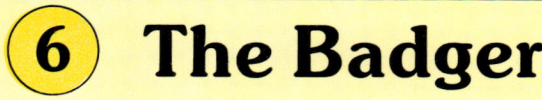

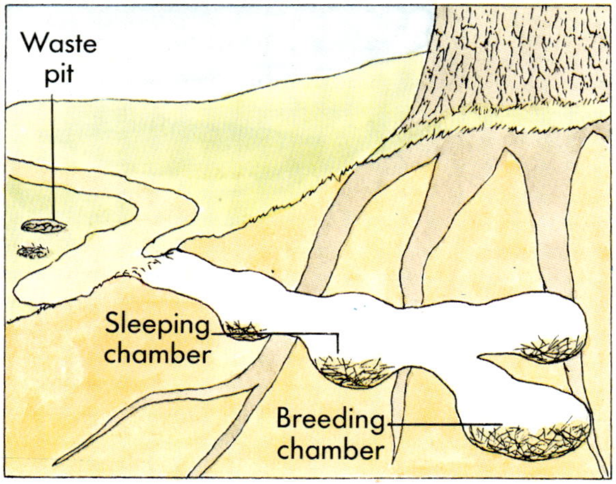

Both the European badger and its cousin the American badger are quite common, but you have probably never seen one. The reason is that they live underground, and only come out to hunt after sunset.

If you look carefully below trees and near earthy banks you might find a badger's home or sett. Look for scratch marks on tree trunks, and scuffed-up earth. Tracks may lead to a number of large holes which are the entrances to the sett.

Badgers are easy to recognize. They have a black and white head, and a greyish coat with black underneath.

Waste pit

Sleeping chamber

Breeding chamber

The badger's body is shaped so that it can dig in soil. The legs are short and strong, and the front feet have long claws. These are used for burrowing and scraping. The sett is added to every year, until it is a maze of underground tunnels and chambers. It is in these chambers that the badgers sleep and give birth to their young.

14

Badgers keep a clean home. Waste matter is buried in a pit outside. The bracken and straw that they sleep on is changed regularly. When the time comes for giving birth, the female fills a special chamber with fresh bedding.

The young are born early in the year, around February. The tiny creatures are blind for over a month. Since they are mammals, they feed on their mother's milk. By the summer they are eating worms and other solid foods. Their eyesight gets better and they have a good sense of smell and hearing. The badger cubs stay with their mother until autumn, when they are old enough to look after themselves.

On summer evenings the badger cubs come out to play. They like to chase in and out of the trees. They try to push each other over, rolling and biting excitedly. These games help them to learn to hunt and grow strong.

As a hunter, the badger is a bit of a slowcoach. It will eat all sorts of things. It hunts worms, snails, insects and small creatures such as mice and voles. But it likes berries and acorns too.

Food is scarce in the winter months. The badger spends much of the time asleep in one of its underground chambers. On warmer days it will sometimes get up, to see if it can find some food.

The golden eagle is a bird of the wide open spaces. It is found in the mountains of Europe, from Scotland down to Spain, in North Africa and Asia, and in North America.

It is a large, powerful creature, with a savage, hooked beak for tearing at its prey. It sweeps down mountain valleys and picks out hares and ptarmigan for the kill. Gripping them in its talons, it soars back to its nest. Golden eagles will also hunt smaller birds and mice. Dead deer and sheep provide a welcome meal during the winter or on bare hills where there is little prey.

The fluffy down which covers the surviving chick soon gives way to proper feathers. At about nine or ten weeks old, the young eagle takes its first flight. Its parents will teach it how to use its sharp talons to hunt live prey.

The young eagles have some white feathers in their wings and tail. Not until they are five years old do they become full adults, with golden-brown feathers all over. With a wingspan of over 2 metres, a golden eagle can patrol a hunting area of 50 square kilometres. An eagle on the wing is a truly magnificent sight.

The golden eagle's nest is called an eyrie. It is built from sticks and is lined with leafy stems. The nest is usually perched on a high rock or in the branches of a tall pine tree safely hidden from its enemies.

The adult eagles, who pair for life, normally produce two eggs. When the chicks hatch out they are fed by the parents. One of the chicks is often killed by the other in the first few weeks of its life.

Talon

8 The Kangaroo

The kangaroo is one of the world's oddest creatures. It has long, powerful rear legs, small forelegs, and a long tail which helps it to keep its balance as it leaps along.

Kangaroos are only found in Australia. The largest and best-known kinds are the red and the grey. A male is often 2 metres tall.

Kangaroos wander in groups, or mobs, of a dozen or so. Sometimes they are attacked by wild dogs called dingoes. If a kangaroo is cornered it can put up a good fight, kicking and slashing with its claws. Male kangaroos fight each other too, usually when a female is ready to mate.

Kangaroos belong to a group of mammals called *marsupials,* which give birth in an unusual way. A baby kangaroo is born after only five weeks inside its mother. The tiny creature at once crawls up into a pouch on its mother's belly.

The baby spends the next ten months in the pouch. Here it is warm and safe. A supply of milk feeds the baby, and it grows all the time. The mother can keep the pouch closed tightly with her muscles. Only one baby is carried at a time.

At last the baby is ready to come out from the pouch. It carries on drinking its mother's milk for another six months. If danger threatens, it climbs back into the pouch. These young kangaroos are called joeys.

Red kangaroos breed all year round and as they have few natural enemies there are large numbers of them. They feed mostly on grass. Many farmers think of kangaroos as pests. The kangaroos often graze on the land the farmers keep for their sheep. Fences will not keep the kangaroos out and so large numbers of them are shot each year.

The kangaroo's powerful hind legs allow it to spring over obstacles such as fences. It can jump to a height of nearly 2 metres and a single bound may cover as much as 13 metres in length. Kangaroos can keep up a speed of 50 kilometres an hour for long periods.

9 The Chimpanzee

The world's trees provide a home for all kinds of wildlife. The dense forests and the mountainsides of central Africa are the home of the chimpanzees. These highly intelligent mammals are apes, first cousins of the gorillas and our nearest relatives in the animal world.

The chimpanzees spend much of their time in the trees. They leap from branch to branch, using all of their four limbs to cling on. In a particular area there may be sixty or so animals, split into troops of between four and fifteen members. Each troop is led by one of the older male chimpanzees. Within a troop there are strong feelings between relatives. Chimps care for each other in a way that seems almost human. They groom each other to clean their coats of irritating insects. They kiss and touch a great deal. But, like humans, they also have a temper.

Chimpanzees feed on fruit, leaves and bark. They also eat termites and ants, and will sometimes attack and eat larger animals. By day they venture into forest clearings and open spaces in search of food.

The 'chimp' has narrow, deft hands. It can strip leaves from a twig, poke it into a termites' nest, and fish out the insects which cling to it.

When we see the way chimps behave, we can hardly help wondering if this was how our first ancestors lived. The apes sometimes use sticks as simple weapons to attack another animal. They walk partly on four legs, and partly on two.

When night falls, the chimpanzees return to the trees. Each night they build a sleeping platform of leaves and branches. By preparing a new bed every time, they avoid the risk of it being infested by insects.

Chimpanzee's brains are one-third the size of our own, but they are very intelligent indeed. Scientists have found that they can communicate with chimps – not by talking, but by using gestures and expressions.

⑩ The African Elephant

The African elephant is so huge that it need not fear any other creature. It is the largest land animal in the world, standing about 4 metres high and weighing six tonnes or so. Although it looks such an awkward animal, it can move very fast, reaching speeds of up to 40 kilometres per hour.

The elephant has a tough, grey skin, and it lumbers through the bush on four great pillars of legs. Two of its teeth have developed into curved tusks, which it uses to uproot trees. Its long trunk is used to pluck leaves, to carry food to the mouth, to breathe — and to squirt water over itself! Elephants come to waterholes to bathe and drink every day. They also enjoy dust bathing and wallowing in mud.

For all their size, elephants are gentle and intelligent creatures. They live in large family groups of twelve or more. Some herds are much bigger. The female, or cow, gives birth two years after mating. The baby, or calf, is well looked after and fiercely defended. An elephant is grown up at fifteen years of age, and lives to be fifty or more.

Elephants eat vast amounts of vegetation every day and can cause great damage to forests. They need a large area of land to live in. A hundred years ago fewer people lived in Africa and there was plenty of room for the elephants. Today there are many towns and farms. The only place where elephants can wander freely is in the national parks.

Many African countries have national parks. Wardens patrol the parks to protect the wildlife. Even so, many elephants are killed by poachers. The poachers take the tusks, which provide ivory. This is used to make jewellery and trinkets, and it is worth a lot of money. Only one-fifth of all the elephants in Africa enjoy protection. It would be a terrible thing if the mighty elephant died out because of our greed.

11 The Lion

The lion, like the elephant, lives in a shrinking world. Once upon a time, lions were to be found throughout Africa and in many parts of Asia. Only one small group still survives in Asia. Most lions now live on the plains of Africa, where there are still large herds of other animals for them to hunt.

The lion is a mammal and belongs to the cat family. Although it weighs some 200 kilograms, its way of life is not so very different from a humble farm cat. It is a meat eater which hunts live prey. After a big meal, the lion stretches out, in the shade of a large tree and dozes.

In the wild, lions live in groups known as prides. The male is a magnificent creature with a long mane. It is easy to see why he is known as the king of beasts. But in fact it is the female, the lioness, which is the best hunter. The male is rather lazy!

A lioness gives birth to two or three cubs as a rule. They feed on milk until they are able to be taught to hunt for themselves. The cubs leave their parents when they are about two or three years old. Most wild lions live to be about fourteen years old, although some live to be twenty or more.

Lions normally kill grass eaters as their prey — antelope such as the wildebeest, or zebra. Lions are cunning hunters, skilled at ambush. They prefer to hunt as a group. Lionesses hide in long grass or scrub, while other members of the pride distract the herd. Suddenly the herd senses trouble and starts galloping around in a panic. However, by this time it is too late — the hunt has already begun.

The black and white stripes of the zebra's hide serve to confuse the lioness in the stampede. Even so, a victim is picked out and felled in a single bound.

When the kill has been made, the herd calms down, and a mighty roar calls the other members of the pride to the feast. The dead animal is soon torn apart and eaten.

When the lions have had their fill, it is the turn of other creatures to eat the remains. Hyenas and vultures pick over the bones. The lions leave to sleep in the shade.

12 The Nile Crocodile

The Nile is one of the great rivers of the world. It carries water from the mountains and lakes of central Africa northwards to the Mediterranean Sea. On its journey it winds through a maze of swamps and sandbanks. This is the home of a reptile which looks like a prehistoric monster – the Nile crocodile.

Nile crocodiles vary in length from 3½ to 5 metres. They have short legs and long, powerful tails. Their bodies are covered in leathery scales coloured brown or green. Their green eyes are set low over a long snout. A crocodile has sixty-six sharp teeth, set around an orange-coloured mouth. Swimming low in the water, the crocodile can be mistaken for a floating log.

'Crocs' spend most of the day lying on the river banks basking in the hot sun. Once in a while they take a dip or open their jaws wide to cool off. Sometimes plovers can be seen perching in the gaping jaws, picking food scraps from the teeth! By night the croc is a hunter. Fish are its main food, but it also attacks birds, cattle, antelope – and humans.

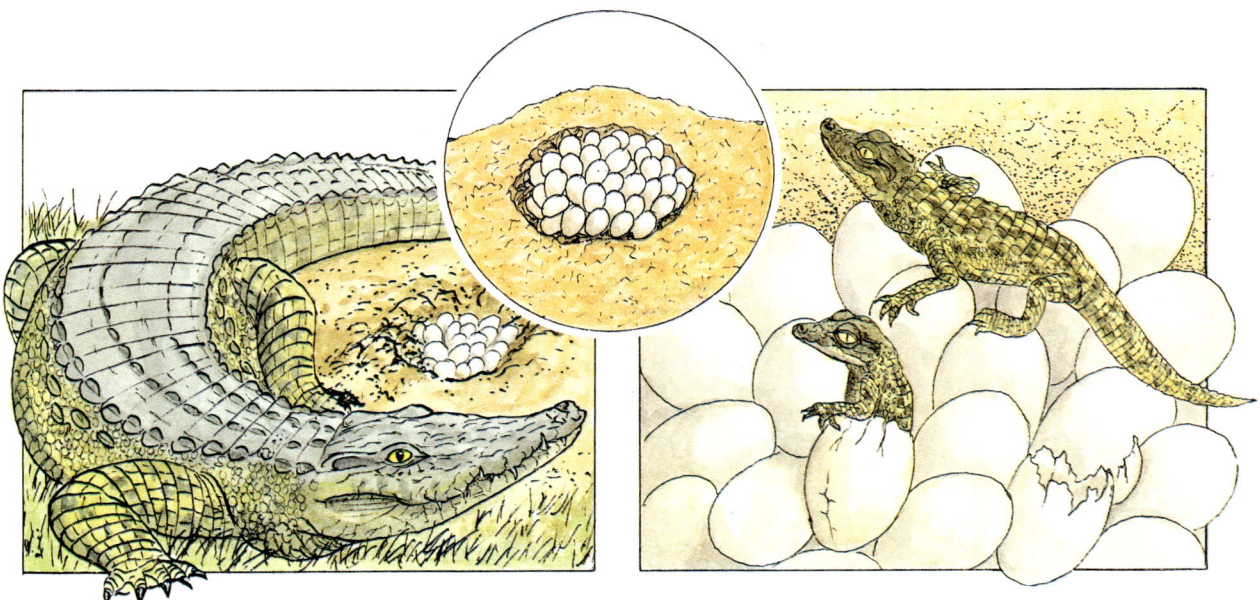

When the female crocodile has mated she finds a sandbank and scoops out a nest about a ½ metre deep. Here she lays up to 50 eggs and covers them with soil. She stays nearby, guarding the nest fiercely. To some lizards and mongooses, crocodile eggs make a very tasty meal.

After about twelve weeks the eggs are ready to hatch. The shell cracks and an 'egg-tooth' on the snout of the baby breaks through the egg lining. This 'tooth' later drops off. The babies make grunting noises and the mother opens the nest. The babies wriggle out, miniature versions of adult crocodiles.

The youngsters clamber all over their mother, who will carry them in her jaws to the river. Soon however she leaves her brood, and they must learn to look after themselves. The babies are often gobbled up by marabou and other birds, and even by adult crocodiles. The lucky survivors grow up slowly, becoming fully-grown adults at about ten years old.

In North Africa and the Middle East are some of the world's last wildernesses — the Sahara, the Nubian and Syrian deserts, and the Rub al Khali, the 'empty quarter' of Saudi Arabia. These are vast areas of rock and shifting sands. By night it is cold and by day the sun burns down fiercely. Water is very scarce.

One of the few animals able to survive these conditions is the Arabian camel, or dromedary. Tame camels are bred by the nomads and traders who cross the desert from one water hole, or oasis, to another. The female gives birth to only one baby at a time. The young camel lives on its mother's milk for a whole year.

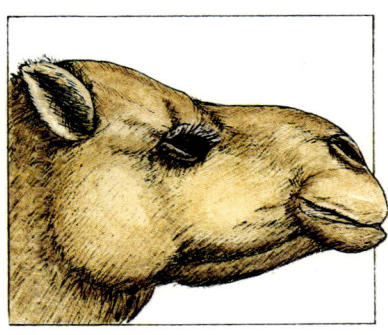

The camel's body has become specially suited to desert life. Small ears and thick eyelashes help keep out blowing sand and the flat nostrils can be closed.

The foot of the camel has two large toes. It is wide, so that it does not sink into soft sand. Thick pads protect the sole from heat, thorns and sharp stones.

The Arabian camel has a single hump on its back. This acts as a food store. Its fat keeps the camel alive when there is a shortage of food and water.

The adult camel is rather a grumpy creature. It grunts and grumbles and often objects to carrying loads that are too heavy. In the mating season males are particularly dangerous, fighting each other and snapping viciously with their powerful jaws.

Despite all this, the camel is one of our most useful beasts of burden. A loaded camel can travel 40 kilometres a day without any problem, only taking a drink every three or four days. Camels can travel for long periods without a rest. Loaded camels often cross deserts in long strings called caravans.

In the last century, Europeans took Arabian camels to Australia. In 1861, the explorers Robert O'Hara Burke and William John Wills died on their expedition across the unknown continent. They had set out with sixteen camels. Camels were also used during the building of the railways in Australia. Descendants of these beasts now run wild. Camels also roam wild in Africa. They too are descended from tame camels.

The coast of Antarctica is one of the loneliest places on Earth. The great stretches of ice and snow are lashed by bitter winds. Few living things can survive here. Yet this is the home of the emperor penguin.

At the beginning of winter at the frozen south pole, the emperor penguins travel inland to breed. The female lays a single egg. If eggs are to hatch out they must be kept warm, and this poses a problem in the harsh Antarctic winter. The emperor penguins have found a solution. The female passes the egg to the male, who places it on his feet. The folds of his belly keep the egg warm until it hatches out.

The female now leaves for the ocean, spending two months feeding. The male stays at home, facing up to the bitter cold without any food. Males huddle together in large groups.

When the egg hatches the male feeds the chick with a liquid from the 'crop' in his throat. At last the female returns to take over the care of the baby penguin. She finds her way back to the exact spot without fail.

The male can now go off to sea and feed until it has put back the fat it lost. As the chick grows up it leaves the shelter of the adult and both parents can bring it food.

While waiting for food the chicks huddle together for warmth and protection. Many die in blizzards, or are attacked by skuas.

When fully grown the emperor penguin is a beautiful bird. It stands nearly 120 centimetres tall and is the largest of the penguins. It is protected from the cold by a layer of fat and by short, sleek feathers.

On land it might seem clumsy. It is unable to fly and waddles around comically. In the sea it is very different. The useless wings are now flippers, and the whole body is streamlined for fast swimming. It needs to be fast to catch the squid and fish it lives on.

The emperor penguin can dive deeper than any other bird in the world. One has been recorded as reaching a depth of 265 metres.

Index